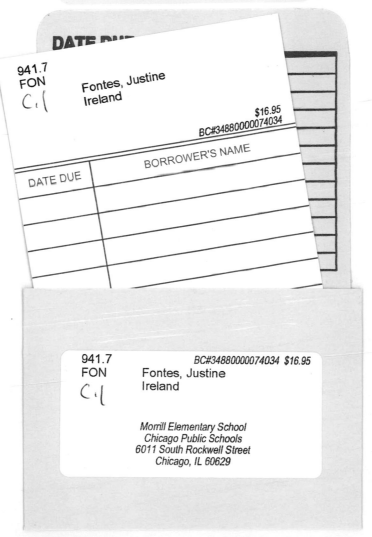

A to Z Ireland

BY JUSTINE AND RON FONTES

children's press®

A Division of Scholastic Inc.
New York Toronto London Auckland Sydney
Mexico City New Delhi Hong Kong
Danbury, Connecticut

Series Consultant: Linda D. Bullock, Ph.D.
Series Design: Marie O'Neill
Photo Research: Candlepants Incorporated

The photos on the cover shows a thatched cottage (right), a sheep (bottom right), an Irish boy (middle), and a patch of clover (left).

Photographs © 2003: Corbis Images: 17, 35 (Bettmann), 9 bottom, 24 top right, 25 top left, 26, 27 left, 34 bottom (Richard Cummins), 10 bottom (Pat Doyle), 31 bottom (Ric Ergenbright), 9 top, 10 top (Charles Gupton), 15 left (Hulton-Deutsch Collection), 16 bottom (Alen MacWeeney), 28 top (Stephanie Maze), 12 bottom, 14, 15 right (Reuters NewMedia Inc.), 5 top right (Lynda Richardson), 12 top (Sean Sexton Collection), 24 bottom (Paul A. Souders), 16 top, 23, 25 top right, 29, 30 (Michael St. Maur Sheil), 36 (Geray Sweeney), 24 top left, 25 bottom (David Turnley), 8 bottom, 28 bottom (Peter Turnley), 31 top (Patrick Ward), 13 (Adam Woolfitt), 32; Dembinsky Photo Assoc.: 4 (Dominique Braud), 7; Envision/Steven Mark Needham: 11; Getty Images/Digital Vision: 18, 19; H. Armstrong Roberts, Inc./M. Diggin: 8 top; Hulton|Archive/Getty Images/Humphrey Spender: 33; ImageState: cover top right (Ron Sanford), cover center; MapQuest.com, Inc.: 21; PhotoDisc/Getty Images/Robert Glusic: cover top left; PictureQuest/Photo 24/Brand X Pictures: cover bottom right; Stone/Getty Images: 6 right, 6 left (Oliver Benn), 27 right (Robin Smith), 34 top (Tom Till), 5 bottom right (Chris Warbey); The Image Bank/Getty Images: 5 top left, 22 (Will & Deni McIntyre), 37 (Topham Picturepoint).
Map by XNR Productions

Library of Congress Cataloging-in-Publication Data
Fontes, Justine.
  Ireland / by Justine and Ron Fontes.
      p. cm. – (A to Z)
Includes bibliographical references and index. Contents: Animals – Buildings – Cities – Dress – Exports – Food – Government – History – Important people – Jobs – Keepsakes – Land– Map – Nation – Only in Ireland – People – Question – Religion – School and sports – Transportation – Unusual places – Visiting the country – Window to the past – X-tra special things – Yearly festivals – Z – Let's explore more – Meet the authors – Gaelic and English words you know.
  ISBN 0-516-24561-9 (lib. bdg.)   0-516-26810-4 (pbk.)
1. Ireland–Juvenile literature. [1. Ireland.] I. Fontes, Ron. II. Title. III. Series.
  DA906.F66   2003
  941.7'003–dc21   2003003703

Contents

Connemara Pony

Animals

Horses and sheep graze in Ireland's beautiful green fields. Other animals live in Ireland, too, including seals, otters, and stoats.

Sheep

Ospreys

One small horse is the Connemara pony. They are very strong. People ride them and use them to do farm work.

Ospreys are birds that dive in the water feet first. They use their sharp claws to grab fish to carry back to their nests. Ospreys build their nests in tall trees.

Irish Setters live in Ireland, too. They are hunting dogs. They work in the fields to bring back birds for hunters.

A stoat, or weasel, has a long body covered with silky fur. You can find stoats living along the riverbanks. They hunt for small animals like rabbits.

Because of their red fur, Irish Setters are sometimes called Red Setters.

Blarney Castle

Buildings

Storefronts like these are in many of Ireland's cities.

Ireland has many castles. Blarney Castle is one of the most popular buildings in Ireland. It is located in the city of Cork. In 1446, it was rebuilt by Dermot McCarthy, the king of Munster. The thick walls have turrets. These are small towers where soldiers hid and watched for enemies during battle.

Cities

Dublin is the largest city and it is also Ireland's capital. About one-fourth of the people live in and around Dublin.

Dublin is the center of Irish business and culture. There is much to see and do there. People shop on O'Connell Street. They sit in parks like St. Stephen's Green. They go to churches, museums, theaters, and gardens.

There are many small villages, too. There are cities like Kilkenny that have castles and old buildings. There are also cities like Waterford, Ireland's main seaport.

O'Connell Street is Dublin's main and busiest street. It has many shops and restaurants.

These girls wear special costumes to perform step dances.

Dress

Dancers often wear fancy costumes when they perform Irish dances. At school, students wear uniforms. At home, many young people wear blue jeans and t-shirts.

Irish people make sweaters by hand and by machine.

The warm waters of the Gulf Stream help keep Ireland warm in the winter, but people still wear sweaters. The Irish use sheep's wool to make thick sweaters. They also weave tweed, a cloth made from more than one color of wool. Tweed is used to make jackets, skirts, pants, and caps.

Exports

Farms cover most of Ireland. Farmers use much of the land for grazing their cows, sheep, and horses. They grow enough food for Ireland and to sell to other countries. They sell dairy products, or foods like cheese and milk. They also sell meats like beef and pork.

The Irish sell sheep's wool and cloth made from wool to other countries. They also export computers, chemicals, oatmeal, and beer.

Irish Oatmeal Recipe

WHAT YOU NEED:
- 5 cups water
- 1 teaspoon salt
- 1 cup Irish oatmeal
- dark brown sugar
- cream or milk

HOW TO MAKE IT:
Bring water and salt to a boil. Slowly stir in oats. Return to boil. Reduce heat and simmer uncovered for 30 minutes, stirring often. Add sugar and cream to taste.

Food

Potatoes are an important part of Irish cooking. So are cabbage, bacon, and mutton, the meat that comes from sheep.

Oatmeal is a favorite, too. Ask an adult to help you make some using the recipe above.

Eamon de Valera was Ireland's prime minister for 21 years.

Government

Ireland has a president, a **prime minister**, and a **parliament**. People in the parliament make laws for the country.

Voters elect, or choose, the president, who may serve twice. Each term lasts seven years.

The president chooses the prime minister, who leads the parliament. The prime minister may serve once, for five years.

Mary McAleese is Ireland's president today.

A farmer picking potatoes

History

One of the worst times in Ireland's history was the Potato **Famine** in the 1800s. At the time, most people were farmers. They did not own their own land. The farmers paid rent using most of what they grew. They fed their families with the food that was left.

Because they were poor, farm families ate mostly potatoes. In 1845, the potato plants died from disease. There were no crops for three years. Millions of people died from hunger. Many left Ireland and went to the United States.

Important People

Many famous writers and musicians have come from Ireland. People also enjoy traditional Irish music and dance all over the world.

(above) Sharon, Jim, Andrea, and Caroline Corrs grew up in the small town of Dundalk. The Corrs started performing in local pubs and now are international stars.

William Butler Yeats

Bono's real name is Paul David Hewson. He lives in Dublin.

Leabhar

(leer)
means book
in Gaelic.

William Butler Yeats was an Irish poet. He and Lady Gregory founded the Abbey Theatre in Dublin in 1904. Today, actors perform the plays of old and new Irish writers there. Another writer was Bram Stoker. He wrote the story *Dracula*.

There are also famous musicians like The Chieftains who play old and new Irish music. Bono is the leader of U2, a popular Irish rock band.

These children are learning to use computers.

Jobs

Although farms cover much of Ireland, most people work in cities and towns. Many work in offices, especially in the computer industry. Technology has become a big part of Ireland's present and future, although there are many small businesses still owned by families.

Stone masons

Keepsakes

There are many stories about St. Patrick, Ireland's **patron saint**. One story says St. Patrick drove all the snakes out of Ireland and into the sea, and that's why there are no snakes in Ireland.

Since the shamrock is the national symbol of Ireland, it decorates many keepsakes. It is also called clover. You can see them on this postcard. This small plant has three leaves. Many people wear a shamrock on St. Patrick's Day.

This postcard shows a picture of St. Patrick. March 17 is St. Patrick's Day and a national holiday.

Steep cliffs line Ireland's west coast.

Lough

(lok)
in Gaelic, means lake.

Land

The green, grassy fields of Ireland gave it the nickname "The Emerald Isle."

Ireland is an island in the North Atlantic Ocean. Most of the central part of Ireland is grassy land. Hills and mountains circle the land. Ireland's tallest mountain is Carrauntoohill. It is part of the Kerry Mountains. Other mountains are the Donegal Mountains, the Mayo Mountains, the Connemara Mountains, where the wild ponies live.

The Shannon River is Ireland's longest river. There are also many lakes, including Lough Allen, Lough Ree, and Lough Derg.

IRELAND

SCOTLAND

ENGLA

NORTHERN
IRELAND
⭐ Belfast

Isle
of
Man

IRELAND

Connemara
National Park

Clifden ■

Galway ●

Dublin ⭐

Irish
Sea

ENGLA

Shannon River

ATLANTIC
OCEAN

Limerick ●

Waterford ●

St. George's Channel

WALES

Cork ●

ENGLAN

N
W ◀ ⦿ ▶ E
S

Map

MILES
0 ———————— 100
KILOMETERS
0 ———————— 100

Nation

Coat of Arms

A country often has symbols that have special meaning to it. Ireland's coat of arms shows a harp, a musical instrument.

Ireland, or the Republic of Ireland, is an independent country. Northern Ireland is part of the United Kingdom of Great Britain which includes Scotland, England, and Wales.

Ninety-two percent of the people in Ireland are Catholic. So are almost half of the people in Northern Ireland. Most other people in Northern Ireland are **Protestant**.

The flag of Ireland has one green, one white, and one orange stripe. The green stripe stands for Catholics. The orange stripe stands for Protestants. The white stripe stands for unity, or the hope of peace among all Irish people.

Only in Ireland

Capall

(COP-uhl) means horse in Gaelic.

You can change the way the bodhrán sounds. It depends on how you play it.

Many Irish believe that the best way to raise great horses is by using kind words. Some also believe that horses enjoy music. That's good, because many Irish people who love horses also love to make music.

In traditional music, you can hear harps, pipes, banjos, flutes, fiddles, and drums. The **bodhrán** is an Irish drum. It is covered in goatskin but is also made with a plastic top. People play this drum with a stick called a beater.

People

Irish people have many different **ancestors**. They include Celts, **Normans**, **Vikings**, and **Britons**.

"Cead mile failte"
(KADE MEE-lah FWAHLT-chuh)
is an Irish greeting that means "a hundred thousand welcomes."

Many people in Ireland's cities live in row houses like these (left). The man above is fixing a thatched roof.

Long ago, the Celts came to Ireland from Europe. The Normans came from France. Bold explorers called Vikings came from Denmark, Norway, and Sweden. Britons came from an island next to Ireland. All of these groups of people settled in Ireland over thousands of years.

There are two official languages in Ireland. They are English and Irish. Irish is another name for the **Gaelic** language spoken in Ireland. The Celts brought this language to Ireland in about 500 B.C.

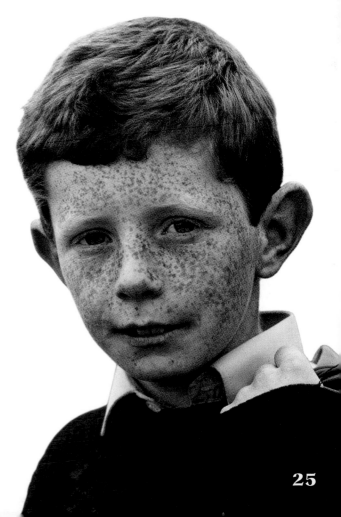

Question
What is the Blarney Stone?

Someone with the gift of **blarney** knows how to get their way. Blarney is another word for sweet talk.

Some people believe there is a magic stone in Blarney Castle. Anyone who kisses the stone is given the gift of blarney. It isn't easy to kiss the stone. Someone must hold the person. The person bends backward over the castle wall until he or she reaches the stone.

Religion

The four-leaf clover is supposed to be lucky.

St. Patrick brought Christianity to Ireland in the 5th century A.D. When he was a boy, pirates took Patrick from his home in England. He became a slave in Ireland. After six years, Patrick escaped and went back to England.

Because of his life in Ireland, Patrick decided to become a **priest**. He returned to Ireland to build churches. St. Patrick's Cathedral in Dublin is Ireland's largest cathedral.

One legend says St. Patrick used the three leaves of the shamrock to teach the Irish about the three forms of the Christian God.

Shamrock is a name used for many types of clover. Sometimes a clover plant grows with four leaves instead of three.

27

Hurling is one of Ireland's favorite sports.

School & Sports

All children from age 6 to 15 must go to school. The Catholic Church runs most schools.

There are lots of games to keep children busy after school. Children and adults play soccer, but in Ireland, it is called *football*. Gaelic football is like soccer, but players can hold the ball.

Men play the old Irish game called hurling. Women play camogie. Both games are like field hockey. There is also boxing, **rugby**, golfing, and more. People enjoy the Irish Derby, too. It is one of the most famous horse races in the world.

Transportation

Buses and trains take most people where they want to go. People also drive cars and ride bicycles. In most villages, walking is the best way to get around.

Dublin Airport is Ireland's busiest airport. Aer Lingus is the national airline. Its symbol is the Irish shamrock.

The shamrock is also the symbol of Ireland's ferries. Fast ferry boats carry people and cars between Ireland and Great Britain. Other ferries travel to and from France.

Because Ireland is an island, shipping is very important.

Unusual Places

The Burren is a rocky place in County Clare where most trees can't grow.

Small plants sprout, and flowers bloom in cracks in the rocks. Visitors go here to see ancient forts and tombs called **dolmens**. A dolmen has a flat, stone top that sits on two or more standing stones. There are also ruins of early Christian churches and castles.

More than twenty kinds of butterflies live in the Burren along with swans, skylarks, and cuckoos.

Many tourists enjoy whale watching. This boat is in Dingle Bay, County Kerry.

Visiting the Country

Below the cliffs in Northern Ireland, a long line of rock columns stretch into the sea. There are about 40,000 columns in all. Most have six sides. Others have four, five, eight, or ten sides. The columns fit together, making a causeway, or path.

People who tried to explain how this unusual path formed told the story of a giant named Finn MacCool. They said the giant built the path to reach his sweetheart in Scotland. That is why today, the path is called the Giant's Causeway.

Before there were electric machines, women used spinning wheels to make yarn.

Window to the Past

Turning wool into cloth and clothing has been a home business in Ireland for a long time.

These women are making fishing nets in a rope factory.

Once a sheep is sheared, the wool is washed and combed into separate strands. The strands are twisted together to make yarn.

Long ago, woolen sweaters were especially important to families on the Aran Islands. Fishermen wore them to stay warm while they worked. Each fisherman's family had its own sweater pattern. Families used the pattern to identify fishermen who drowned. Today, people can buy Aran sweaters all over Ireland.

Many ancient carvings have faces on both sides: One to see the future and the other to watch the world of humans.

X-tra Special Things

St. Matthew

Ireland is famous for stories and legends. One such legend says that if you catch a leprechaun, he will lead you to a pot of gold. Visitors laugh at signs posted in Killarney National Park. The signs say "Leprechaun Crossing."

One of the most famous and beautiful books (above) in the world is *The Book of Kells*. Irish monks wrote and decorated the book by hand more than one thousand years ago. The book tells stories from the Bible.

Yearly Festivals

When Irish musicians perform, lots of people join in. People play music in **pubs** and on the street.

These musicians are performing at a music festival in Ballina (left).
These children are getting ready to march in a St. Patrick's Day parade (above).

Irish people celebrate many religious holidays. Christmas, Easter, and Lent are a few. Families spend the holidays together.

They also celebrate St. Brigid's Day on February 1. Long ago, this day marked the change in weather as winter turned into spring. When Christianity came, St. Brigid's Day became a holy day. People put crosses made from straw above their doors. The crosses were said to keep houses safe from harm and bring blessings from St. Brigid.

Aa bb Cc Ɔd
ee ꝼf Ꟗg ꜧh 1i
Ll mm nn Oo
ꝑp Rr Ss Ꞇt Uu

Z

The kind of Gaelic spoken in Ireland is called Irish. The letter Z is not in the Irish alphabet. Neither are J, K, Q, V, W, X, and Y.

The Irish language almost died out after people from England invaded Ireland almost one thousand years ago. Then in the late 1880s, writers began to use Irish again. It became one of Ireland's official languages in 1922.

Today, children learn both Irish and English in school. About one-third of the people speak Irish.

■ Gaelic and English Words

ancestor (AN-sess-tur) a family member who lived long ago

blarney (BLAHR-nee) flattering talk or nonsense

bodhrán (BAN-rahn) Gaelic word for drum

Britons (BRIH-tuhns) the people who lived in Southern England before the Roman Conquest in A.D. 43.

capall (COP-uhl) Gaelic word for horse.

cead mile failte (KADE MEE-lah FWAHLT-chuh) a Gaelic greeting that means a hundred thousand welcomes

dolmen (DOLE-muhn) a tomb made of a big, flat stone laid on top of two large upright stones

famine (FA-muhn) an extreme shortage of food; hunger or starvation

Gaelic (GAY-lik) the Irish language; any of the Celtic languages spoken in Ireland, Scotland, and the Isle of Man

leabhar (leer) Gaelic word for book

lough (lok) Gaelic word for lake

Normans the people living in the Normandy region of northern France during the Middle Ages (from 1000 to A.D. 1453.)

osprey (AHS-pree) a large bird of prey that feeds on fish, also called a fish hawk

parliament (PAHR-luh-muhnt) the part of a government consisting of people elected by the citizens to make laws for their country

patron saint (PAY-truhn saynt) a holy person who guides and protects a living person or a place from heaven

priest (preest) a minister appointed by the Roman Catholic church to perform religious services, like ceremonies, sermons, and weddings

prime minister the head of the government in a country that elects a Parliament

Protestant (PRAH-tuhs-stuhnt) a member of any of the Christian churches that separated from the Roman Catholic Church

pub a public house, the local bar and gathering place in English, Irish, and Scottish towns

rugby an English game like American football, played with an oval ball that can be kicked, carried, or passed from hand to hand

Vikings (VYE-kng) pirates and traders from Denmark, Norway, and Sweden who raided and settled in parts of northwestern Europe from the 8th to 11th centuries

■ Let's Explore More

A Visit to Ireland by Rachel Bell, Heineman Library, 1999

Look What Came From Ireland by Miles Harvey, Franklin Watts, 2002

Brigid's Cloak: An Ancient Irish Story by Bryce Milligan, Wm. B. Eerdmans Publishing, 2002

Websites

www.blarneycastle.ie/
Find out more about Blarney Castle and the Blarney Stone at this website.

www.local.ie/entertainment/
Find out about dance, music, and other kid-friendly things to see and do all over Ireland.

www.homepage.tinet.ie/~whitechurchns/kool_kidz_of_ireland.htm
Learn about Ireland from a site prepared by Irish schoolchildren.

Italic page numbers indicate illustrations.

Meet the Authors

JUSTINE & RON FONTES have written nearly 400 children's books together. Since 1988, they have published *critter news*, a free newsletter that keeps them in touch with publishers from their home in Maine.

The Fonteses have written many biographies and early readers, as well as historical novels and other books combining facts with stories. Their love of animals is expressed in the nature notes columns of *critter news*.

During his childhood in Tennessee, Ron was a member of the Junior Classical League and went on to tutor Latin students. At 16, Ron was drawing a science fiction comic strip for the local newspaper. A professional artist for 30 years, Ron has also been in theater as a costumer, makeup artist, and designer.

Justine was born in New York City and worked in publishing while earning a BA in English Literature Phi Beta Kappa from New York University. Thanks to her parents' love of travel, Justine visited most of Europe as a child, going as far north as Finland. During college, she spent time in France and Spain.